Hal•Leonard

Jazz Play-Along®

Book & Audio for B♭, E♭, C and Bass Clef Instruments

Volume 107

Arranged and Produced
by Mark Taylor

Motown Classics

10 POPULAR HITS

PLAYBACK+
Speed • Pitch • Balance • Loop

To access audio, visit:
www.halleonard.com/mylibrary

8530-2996-9879-4848

ISBN 978-1-4234-5618-6

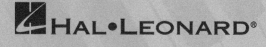

HAL•LEONARD®

Visit Hal Leonard Online at
www.halleonard.com

World headquarters, contact:
Hal Leonard
7777 West Bluemound Road
Milwaukee, WI 53213
Email: info@halleonard.com

In Europe, contact:
Hal Leonard Europe Limited
1 Red Place
London, W1K 6PL
Email: info@halleonardeurope.com

In Australia, contact:
Hal Leonard Australia Pty. Ltd.
4 Lentara Court
Cheltenham, Victoria, 3192 Australia
Email: info@halleonard.com.au

MOTOWN CLASSICS

Volume 107

Arranged and Produced by
Mark Taylor and Jim Roberts

Featured Players:

Graham Breedlove–Trumpet
John Desalme–Tenor Saxophone
Tony Nalker–Piano
Jim Roberts–Guitar
Regan Brough–Bass
Steve Fidyk–Drums

Recorded at Bias Studios, Springfield, Virginia
Bob Dawson, Engineer

HOW TO USE THE AUDIO:

Each song has <u>two</u> tracks:

1) Split Track/Demonstration

Woodwind, Brass, Keyboard, and **Mallet Players** can use this track as a learning tool for melody style and inflection.

Bass Players can learn and perform with this track – remove the recorded bass track by turning down the volume on the LEFT channel.

Keyboard and **Guitar Players** can learn and perform with this track – remove the recorded piano part by turning down the volume on the RIGHT channel.

2) Backing Track

Soloists or **Groups** can learn and perform with this accompaniment track with the RHYTHM SECTION only.

AIN'T NO MOUNTAIN HIGH ENOUGH

WORDS AND MUSIC BY NICKOLAS ASHFORD
AND VALERIE SIMPSON

C VERSION

ALL IN LOVE IS FAIR

WORDS AND MUSIC BY
STEVIE WONDER

C VERSION

DANCING IN THE STREET

C VERSION

WORDS AND MUSIC BY MARVIN GAYE,
IVY HUNTER AND WILLIAM STEVENSON

FOR ONCE IN MY LIFE

WORDS BY RONALD MILLER
MUSIC BY ORLANDO MURDEN

C VERSION

HOW SWEET IT IS
(TO BE LOVED BY YOU)

C VERSION

WORDS AND MUSIC BY EDWARD HOLLAND,
LAMONT DOZIER AND BRIAN HOLLAND

Let's Get It On

WORDS AND MUSIC BY MARVIN GAYE
AND ED TOWNSEND

C VERSION

MY GIRL

WORDS AND MUSIC BY WILLIAM "SMOKEY" ROBINSON
AND RONALD WHITE

Never Can Say Goodbye

WORDS AND MUSIC BY
CLIFTON DAVIS

C VERSION

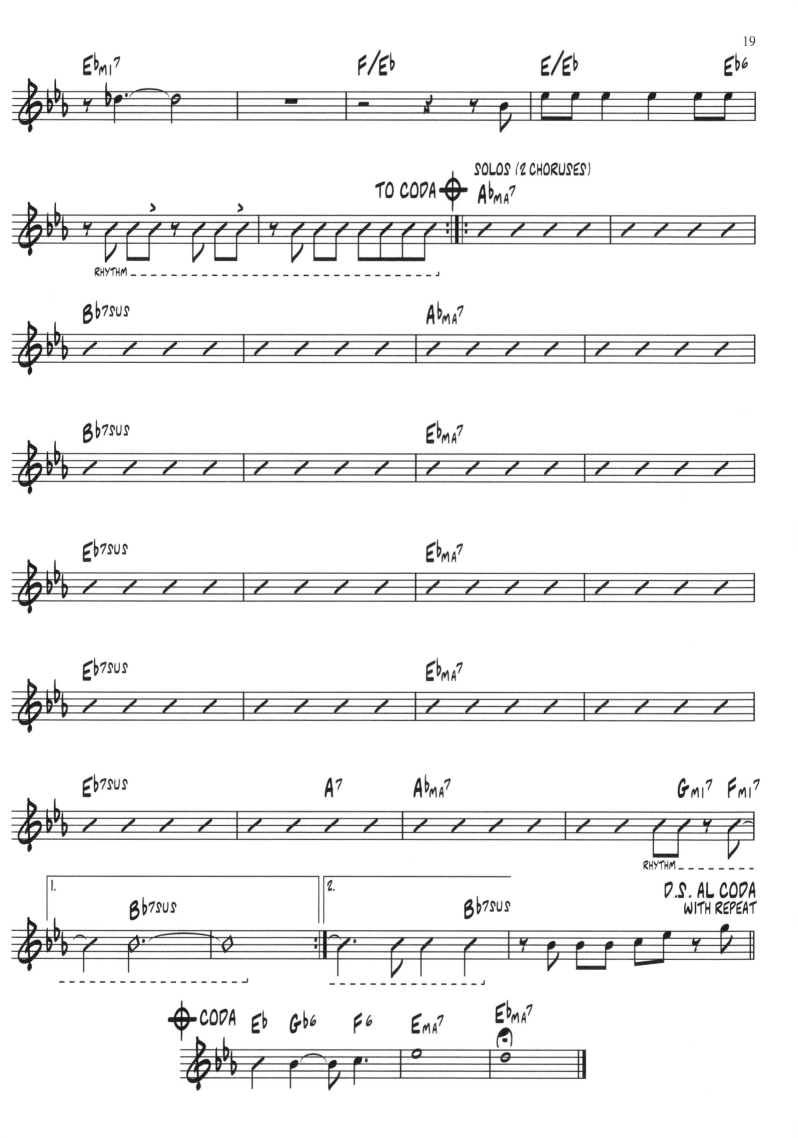

WHAT BECOMES OF THE BROKEN HEARTED

C VERSION

WORDS AND MUSIC BY JAMES A. DEAN, PAUL RISER
AND WILLIAM HENRY WEATHERSPOON

I HEARD IT THROUGH THE GRAPEVINE

WORDS AND MUSIC BY NORMAN J. WHITFIELD
AND BARRETT STRONG

C VERSION

I Heard It Through the Grapevine

WORDS AND MUSIC BY NORMAN J. WHITFIELD
AND BARRETT STRONG

Bb VERSION

Ain't No Mountain High Enough

WORDS AND MUSIC BY NICKOLAS ASHFORD
AND VALERIE SIMPSON

Bb VERSION

ALL IN LOVE IS FAIR

WORDS AND MUSIC BY
STEVIE WONDER

DANCING IN THE STREET

WORDS AND MUSIC BY MARVIN GAYE,
IVY HUNTER AND WILLIAM STEVENSON

Bb VERSION

FOR ONCE IN MY LIFE

WORDS BY RONALD MILLER
MUSIC BY ORLANDO MURDEN

HOW SWEET IT IS
(TO BE LOVED BY YOU)

WORDS AND MUSIC BY EDWARD HOLLAND,
LAMONT DOZIER AND BRIAN HOLLAND

Bb VERSION

Let's Get It On

WORDS AND MUSIC BY MARVIN GAYE
AND ED TOWNSEND

Bb Version

MY GIRL

WORDS AND MUSIC BY WILLIAM "SMOKEY" ROBINSON
AND RONALD WHITE

NEVER CAN SAY GOODBYE

WORDS AND MUSIC BY
CLIFTON DAVIS

WHAT BECOMES OF
THE BROKEN HEARTED

Bb VERSION

WORDS AND MUSIC BY JAMES A. DEAN, PAUL RISER
AND WILLIAM HENRY WEATHERSPOON

Ain't No Mountain High Enough

WORDS AND MUSIC BY NICKOLAS ASHFORD
AND VALERIE SIMPSON

Eb VERSION

ALL IN LOVE IS FAIR

WORDS AND MUSIC BY
STEVIE WONDER

DANCING IN THE STREET

WORDS AND MUSIC BY MARVIN GAYE,
IVY HUNTER AND WILLIAM STEVENSON

Eb VERSION

FOR ONCE IN MY LIFE

WORDS BY RONALD MILLER
MUSIC BY ORLANDO MURDEN

Eb VERSION

HOW SWEET IT IS
(TO BE LOVED BY YOU)

WORDS AND MUSIC BY EDWARD HOLLAND,
LAMONT DOZIER AND BRIAN HOLLAND

Eb VERSION

LET'S GET IT ON

WORDS AND MUSIC BY MARVIN GAYE
AND ED TOWNSEND

Eb VERSION

MY GIRL

WORDS AND MUSIC BY WILLIAM "SMOKEY" ROBINSON
AND RONALD WHITE

Never Can Say Goodbye

WORDS AND MUSIC BY
CLIFTON DAVIS

Eb VERSION

WHAT BECOMES OF
THE BROKEN HEARTED

Eb Version

WORDS AND MUSIC BY JAMES A. DEAN, PAUL RISER
AND WILLIAM HENRY WEATHERSPOON

59

I HEARD IT THROUGH THE GRAPEVINE

WORDS AND MUSIC BY NORMAN J. WHITFIELD
AND BARRETT STRONG

Eb VERSION

I HEARD IT THROUGH THE GRAPEVINE

WORDS AND MUSIC BY NORMAN J. WHITFIELD
AND BARRETT STRONG

C VERSION

SLOW ROCK

Ain't No Mountain High Enough

WORDS AND MUSIC BY NICKOLAS ASHFORD
AND VALERIE SIMPSON

All in Love Is Fair

WORDS AND MUSIC BY
STEVIE WONDER

Dancing in the Street

WORDS AND MUSIC BY MARVIN GAYE,
IVY HUNTER AND WILLIAM STEVENSON

𝄢: C VERSION

FOR ONCE IN MY LIFE

WORDS BY RONALD MILLER
MUSIC BY ORLANDO MURDEN

HOW SWEET IT IS
(TO BE LOVED BY YOU)

WORDS AND MUSIC BY EDWARD HOLLAND,
LAMONT DOZIER AND BRIAN HOLLAND

𝄢 C VERSION

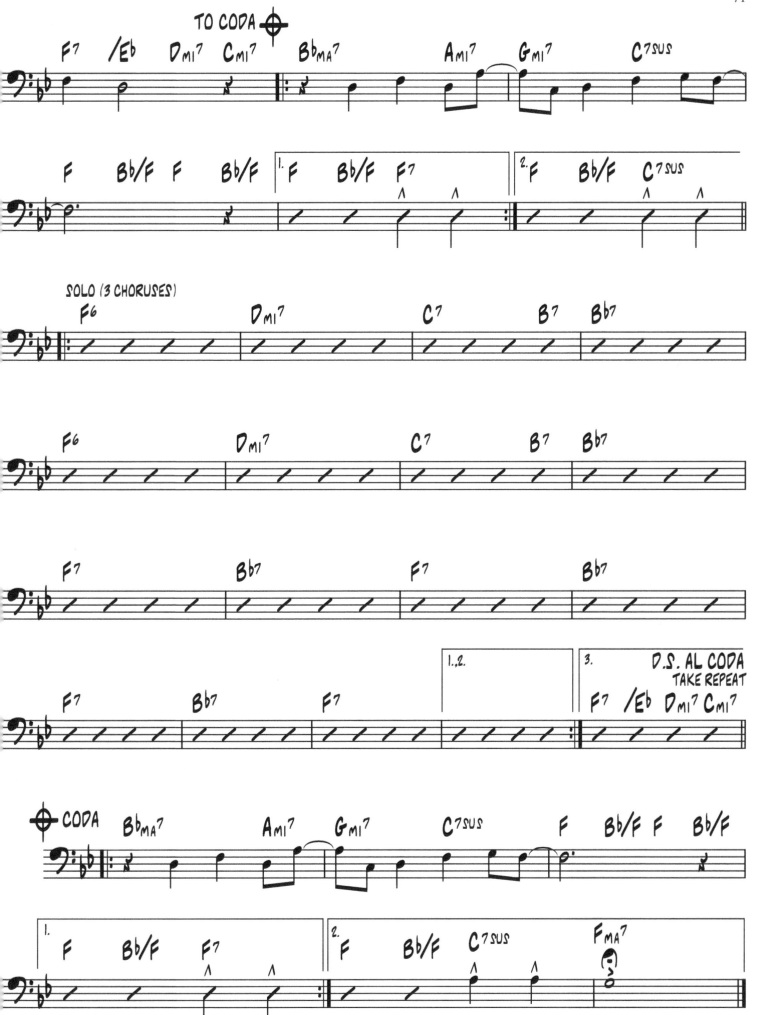

Let's Get It On

WORDS AND MUSIC BY MARVIN GAYE
AND ED TOWNSEND

73

MY GIRL

WORDS AND MUSIC BY WILLIAM "SMOKEY" ROBINSON
AND RONALD WHITE

Never Can Say Goodbye

WORDS AND MUSIC BY
CLIFTON DAVIS

C VERSION

MEDIUM LATIN ROCK

WHAT BECOMES OF
THE BROKEN HEARTED

ℑ: C VERSION

WORDS AND MUSIC BY JAMES A. DEAN, PAUL RISER
AND WILLIAM HENRY WEATHERSPOON